Portrait of a Golf Addict

GEORGE HOUGHTON

HART PUBLISHING COMPANY, INC.

New York City, New York

Contents

GOLF ADDICTS ARE
HUMAN PHENOMENA.

LIKE TROUBLE, THEY CAN
BE FOUND EVERYWHERE.

THE MALE OF THE SPECIES
IS MORE COMMON BUT
LESS DANGEROUS···

A WILD BROTHERHOOD,
THEY SEEM TO ENJOY
THE SAME KIND OF
SELF-INFLICTED PAIN····

PORTRAIT OF A GOLF ADDICT

MORNING ANTICIPATION IS FOLLOWED BY

FIRST-TEE NERVES AND—

ABSURD SENSITIVITY TO BAD SHOTS...

**THE ADDICT HAS A TENDENCY TO TELL LIES
IN THE BAR...**

UTTER LONELINESS IS NORMAL, SO IS —

ABYSMAL DEPRESSION... BUT THERE'S ALWAYS...

THE SURPRISE OF GLORIOUS SUCCESS...

THE ATTRACTIVE POSSIBILITY OF BEING MISTAKEN FOR A TIGER!

TO THE ADDICT, GOLF IS A CHALLENGE —

OF INFINITE VARIETY...

OFTEN THE GAME CAUSES WIFE TROUBLE...

IN BED!

YOUR ADDICT HAS A KEEN SENSE OF URGENCY AND—

HIS ASSESSMENT OF PRIORITIES IS SOUND...

HE DOESN'T BELIEVE IN BAD WEATHER

HE HAS A PROPENSITY FOR HOME STUDY,

TAKES INFINITE CARE...

REMOVES OBSTACLES, LIKE FLIES' WINGS, YET—

**SHORT PUTTS OFTEN REFUSE TO DROP,
DESPITE—**

BRINKMANSHIP!

THINGS GO WRONG, INCREDIBLY...

**SUICIDE IS REGULARLY CONTEMPLATED,
BUT—**

THE INVENTIVE BRAIN WHIRLS...

TO SOLVE ETERNAL PROBLEMS.

THE ADDICT SEES GOLF AS A PLEASANT THING...

CHILDISH JOY FOLLOWS MODEST GAIN...

**BUT THERE'S AN UGLY SIDE...HATRED
SEETHES FOR...**

CHATTERING WOMEN, AND

LOST PENCILS,

**SOCK-TUCKERS-IN, ESPECIALLY IN
FINE WEATHER...**

ONE DAY, WHEN THE WHOLE WORLD
SMILES —

YOUR ADDICT WILL HIT A SNORTER...

LONG PUTTS MAKE SWEET MUSIC...

OCCASIONAL FLUKES...

SPEED HIM ON THE CLOUDS TO STARDOM...

THE CUP OF VICTORY IS FREELY QUAFFED AND—

THE WARM LIMELIGHT OF SUCCESS
SHINES ON THE HERO

GOLF IS BIGGER THAN US ALL

SAGA OF A GOLF ADDICT

I Am Introduced to the Game

MY GOLF CAREER began in a public park. I had been watching an elderly gentleman "limbering up." Never before had I met the phrase. The old man used it to describe hitting a lot of golf balls in more or less the same direction. It appeared to be good fun. As reward for retrieving the balls, I was allowed to hit a ball.

That first brave, scything swipe was astonishly effective. The ball (it nearly hit a nursemaid) went even further than those which had been hit by the limbering-up man.

Something quite extraordinary had happened. No sooner did the clubhead spank the ball than a new kind of glow surged through my veins. As the ball soared, a chemical reaction started up within the adrenalin content of my bloodstream. I didn't realize it then, but my fate was settled for ever. I became a golf addict.

Years have passed, but I often think of that first delicious clout. Pleasant memory has no doubt stretched the distance which the golf ball actually travelled. But maybe not. I think that by pure accident something tremendous clicked.

The mechanism of the movement must have been O.K. I think that in this uninhibited first swing I accidentally discovered the subtle secrets of timing and power. Good golf is fugitive, but that early clean hit has led me to believe that somewhere within my torso, shoulders, forearms, or hands, the secret lies hidden. And the search has always been on since.

When I clipped that first screamer in the park, I was only twelve years old; so it is reasonably certain that according to accepted standards the limbering-up man's golf club was inches too long for me. Believing that this fact may have contributed to the success of the blow, I have often experimented with elongated drivers.

This is the kind of emotional brew that has turned my life into a battlefield.

That swipe in the park was genesis. Within an hour I was back home on the lawn replaying that colossal clout with a cane and a tennis ball. It didn't feel the same. So I tried hitting stones—which was all right until one went through the kitchen window. As I was slipping away, a neighbor beckoned from over the hedge. "Try it with this," he said, handing me an old, wooden-shafted golf club.

I beamed gratitude and accepted what turned out to be an ancient cleek.

Without delay, I returned to the park. The L-U man was still there, sweating and bashing. After retrieving the balls for him I tried hitting them back with my club. That was the second stage. The addiction had developed.

Pebbles at the source changed the course of my life stream. Under other circumstances, no doubt, I would have been interested in model aeroplanes, color photography, messing about with boats, or girls, or planting lettuce beds, or—well, there are many things I could have done. Instead, I simply followed the age-old pattern established by those dedicated to golf.

Before I was fourteen years old, I owned an additional five golf clubs. Realizing there was no hope of dissuading me from my inclination, my father had bought the clubs from a shop selling articles which had been left behind in railway trains. Dad called them "sticks." So hoary were they that it occurred to me later that the articles in question could have probably been sold as museum pieces.

But I was happy to have them. I now owned a putter, a spoon, a niblick, two mashies, and my cleek. They lived in my heart. Smartened up with a lick of varnish and some new twine they became cherished possessions. My golf bag was a present from a friendly garbage collector.

So, from diverse sources, I acquired equipment. The old gentleman in the park helped by supplying two fairly new golf balls.

By agreeing to cut the grass at least twice a week throughout the summer, I had my Dad's permission to make a neat hole in the lawn. But the blemish must be hidden away in a corner, he said, behind a flower-bed and a lilac tree—unusual hazards for my putting practice.

Most of all I enjoyed hitting balls as far as possible in the park. One day—perhaps unfortunately—the L-U man explained the correct way to swing a golf club. He talked pendulums and pivots—and this caused a setback. I realized that golf was not so easy as it had seemed. After about a dozen swings without making contact with the ball, I was so angry that I gathered up my clubs and ran home.

Every forenoon during the long school holiday I took regular doses of golf. The old L-U man (he was really about forty) and I became good friends.

"I like golf better than tennis, or football, or swimming, or camping, or fighting, or . . ."

"Good," interrupted L-U. "Keep at it. With no regrets I've flogged golf for thirty years."

I wondered if the man was joking. He was dead serious. I didn't laugh either.

The Virus Takes Root

EARLY ONE MORNING, when birds were singing and all the world smiled, I stepped on to a golf course for the very first time. It was like walking on steam and I glowed warm with pride. I carried the old bag—which was really why I was there.

"Pay attention and I'll teach you the rules," said my friend.

I should explain that L-U was a southpaw golfer. He attacked the ball from the starboard side, and at that early age I came to appreciate that there are more ways than one of achieving the same result. Left-handed or not, my friend usually hit the ball well.

He cracked a sweet one up the fairway; then as we walked towards his next shot, he outlined the fundamentals. The object was simply to get the ball into the holes by hitting it as seldom as possible. Nothing more; nothing less. Hooks, slices, bogeys, birdies, bunkers, and the like were simply appendages to the game. They could be learned later.

By the 5th hole, I knew how to mark the scorecard, how to hold the flag without letting my shadow fall over the hole, how to cheat by coughing just as the ball is being struck. . . . It was fascinating.

Like the sun, the old man's golf was brilliant (at

53

least I thought so) until we reached the 15th, when his ball swung away to the left and vanished into woods. Somehow, I hadn't ever expected to hear the nice old man say what he did. It came as a mild shock. I realized that at moments like this a golfer forgets everything and everybody. Years of good manners and civilization can peel off in seconds, exposing the savage in the best of us.

L-U growled something which I thought meant he wished me to go and retrieve his ball; but when I trotted off he growled again, and this time I correctly interpreted the noise to mean he wanted another ball from the pocket in his bag.

After the next blow, the ball swirled quickly round to the right and buried itself into the face of a bunker. I wondered what the man could say that could express more anger than before.

But the storm was spent. Quite astonishingly, L-U smiled. "Too much left hand," he murmured, and gently scolded himself. (Later on I would have known that if he had not been left-handed, he would have said: "Too much *right* hand.")

We walked towards the bunker. To my surprise L-U was acutally humming a popular song. I tried a gentle whistle to let him see that I didn't care either.

"All part of the game," said my friend, "like sleepless nights."

Slowly, golf was beginning to sink in.

My First Match

FOR MY FOURTEENTH birthday my father enrolled me as a Junior Member at a neighboring golf club. He thought, no doubt, that this would confine my golf to the proper environment, allowing for more concentration at school.

Strangely enough, my mother had no patience with the scheme. I have an idea her father had been an addict and had treated the family shamefully. Also, Mom had heard that golfers were prone to stomach ulcers, insomnia, and the like.

"The boy seems so young for golf," she whimpered to my father, as if I had enlisted for the militia.

Like a warrior wiping away the sweat of battle, a few days later I returned from my first real game of golf. I had played alone, just a solitary zig-zagging over 18 holes.

It wasn't a great round, but inside I glowed. By the 7th I was playing with abandon, and four of my five repainted balls were lost. The terrain and I were now acquainted.

Better golfers than I would have quit after taking twelve shots from a bunker, but I battled on. My drive and approach at the 18th were peaches. Forget the four putts—they didn't matter.

Back in the clubhouse, to my elderly friend I

breathlessly described every shot. He listened. I had learned another lesson about the give and take of golf talk.

During these early days, I mostly played alone. But I still went out with the limbering-up man who sometimes gave me a stroke a hole, depending on whether or or not he had a good drive from the first tee. Usually, our matches were close and although I enjoyed these encounters, I preferred to wander alone into the wilds of the course to fathom things out. Often I played on after the sun had set. During those dusky hours the roots of my addiction penetrated into rich, fertile soil. The plant developed with uncontrollable growth.

Golf has given me more slaps than kisses. Yet, from those early days I have regarded the game as something terrifyingly important.

I could never understand the folk who consider it otherwise. "I'd like to play, if only I had time . . . ," they say. With me it has been entirely different. I used to say: "I'll do my homework, if I have time after golf."

From my fourteenth birthday, golf has been priority No. 1. If there are insufficient hours on the clock to take care of everything, then demands must take their turn *after* golf. In my timetable, golf never has to be fitted in.

Strange why some people can't take golf more seriously. They talk of "hitting a few holes," as if our game can be taken in large or small doses, as required.

I once had a picture book which contained an illustration of the sport of birling, which is the art of navigating or rolling on logs. Can you imagine a birler saying to his wife: "I'm just going out for a few rolls"? Certainly not. There is a time for birling, just as there are times for breakfast, church, school, work . . . and so on.

Whatever my faults as a boy, I was never guilty of disrespect to golf through casualness. The limbering-up man would never have stood for that.

My pals went to the movies, or ran around with girls. I stayed home, putting on the living-room carpet. Mother worried because I was not like other boys. Dad tried to console her: "He'll grow out of it." But he spoke without conviction, for he was wise and knew a thing or two about people who took to drink, and that.

Climbing is not in my line, but I know how Sir Edmund Hillary felt when he conquered Everest. Soon after my sixteenth birthday, I broke 90.

You won't find my first 89 in the annals of golf. It was scored when I was alone one autumn evening as the light faded. I've kept the card. It's yellow and the pencil marks are wearing away, but it has an honored place—'twixt pages of *How to Play Golf*, by Harry Vardon. I've since played better rounds, of course, but few have been so pleasant. Often, on long winter evenings, during a pause in carpet putting, I take out the card and relive the shots made during that idyllic session. . . . The last putt, a seven-footer, dies into the can at the 18th. . . . The startling realization that at last 90 is broken!

Now to take care of 80! I felt it was just around the corner.

Without more than the usual trials and tribulations, I eventually followed my 89 with an 88, then an 87. At last I was ready for a handicap. Stuff like this would get me a handicap of 16, maybe less.

Three signed cards were required. My first was filled in by a pimply young man with a handicap of 18. I thought it a good idea to play with someone whom I could beat.

The night before, I slept badly. Every possible type of shot was played on my pillow. Several times I woke up, sweating.

Next morning, muttering "Relax! Relax! Relax!". . . I joined my opponent on the first tee. "Relax! Relax! Relax!"

"Ax" sounded in my ears for the first three holes—which was probably why my shots had a chopping action.

Recently I had broken 90 three times. Why not again? "Just play your natural game," I told myself. "Swing easily. Don't worry; don't panic; be normal. Smile. It's only a game. Nothing to be nervous about...."

Long years have passed, but this emotional stuff continues. On the first tee, before an important game, I'm still the terrified youth taking out his first card for a handicap. My hands get damp and I talk too much in that high-pitched voice which is usually a sign of mild hysteria.

On this first-card occasion my opponent, though pimply, was cheery enough. For him, golf was a pleasant social pastime. That sinister fact stood out a mile and made matters worse. I wish that I could always play with folk who feel as I do. It would be a help.

This chap wore his trousers tucked into his socks,

although it wasn't wet, and this habit I have deplored ever since. One glance at a guy like this and I'm so revolted that I always have three or four successive bad shots until I overcome my nausea.

Another thing—he was grinning! I wanted to tell him how serious this outing was—for me at any rate— but I'm almost sure he would have laughed outright.

He'd forgotten to bring a pencil, an omission which could be excused (since, after all, it was my card he was to score), but also, after I had produced a pencil, he calmly asked me to lend him a tee! You may consider these things unimportant, but don't forget that for me this occasion was the culmination of hours of practice and weeks of anxiety.

The ball which Pimples teed up was so gray and tired-looking that I felt ashamed. Yet he smacked it straight and perfectly honestly.

Even before my turn to drive I felt pretty certain that this would not be my day. It wasn't. The ball squittered off the heel of the club and sneaked into the rough. Five more and I was on the green. Three putts made eight. Pimples had registered an orthodox four and infuriated me by saying "Bad luck" when my second putt carefully avoided the hole from a distance of twenty inches. Hole by hole, the torture continued.

At last it was over. I had taken 107. I muttered the usual imbecilities about giving the game up.

My opponent handed me the card. "You won't put this in, will you?" he asked. I had the idea of splitting his pate with my No. 7.

"No. Sorry you've been bothered," I answered.

I Meet the Boss

SINCE THAT DAY of youthful pain (or painful youth) I've learned to fight frustration, seldom victoriously, but nevertheless I'm prepared for it from the start. The surprise has gone. In golfing combat, I now meet pimply perfection with an inward smile, because I know that this type of golfer gets no fun from his skill. I need not be envious. When he clips a good one off the meat, there is no deep enjoyment. Fine golf shots seldom happen to me, but by heaven when they do, I could leap to the moon.

Within an hour of having been carved up, I was back on the course ironing things out. It has been that way ever since, thank goodness. The bug doesn't bite—it gobbles you up. You live with the recurrent thought that the next shot will be the best ever.

I returned to school with a handicap of 20.

Every day, during the holidays I practiced fervently. That wasn't all. At any old time, day or night, I clutched and twisted my fingers in grip exercises. But also there was soul searching, to take care of the mental and spiritual side, and a kind of Yoga drill that a man from Kashmir had told me about for strengthening concentration.

For me, golf was nearly everything. Eating and

sleeping were governed only by the necessities of physical fitness.

On my seventeenth birthday I was able to see my 17 on the handicap board changed to 16.

Then, in the middle of all this happiness, my father asked me to have a word with him in the drawing-room, and I knew something fairly disagreeable was about to happen.

"You're almost a man now," he said. "It's time we gave some thought to your future."

Only for brief moments had the question of a career entered my mind. With golf buzzing around, there was no room for much else.

"Have you given thought as to how you might eventually earn a living?" Dad asked.

Without any warning it was hard to give a snap answer. A travelling salesman with a Scottish firm, perhaps. Based on Carnoustie, or Muirfield, I could play the finest courses in the world. That was roughly the idea. But before I could toss in the suggestion, Dad said: "Well, I haven't really given it much thought either."

Good. Then perhaps there was time to persevere with the technique of getting my right shoulder well under my chin for the follow through. I'd been working on it for days.

Tragically, and it might have been an irreparable setback, the very next evening Dad announced that I was to meet a friend of his who manufactured brushes. He had been to school with Dad; would probably take me on.

At the end of our chat, I was limp and depressed. Dad had troubled on about brushes being a universal product in constant demand, etc.

An interview was arranged, and within a week I went to see the boss of an imposing factory.

Dad's friend received me and shook hands with a firm overlapping grip. I sat down and the man asked about my school and told me about his business. Then, during the latter part of the conversation, which was fairly heavy going, my eye rotated around the room. Suddenly, quite close to where his secretary was sitting, I spotted something which gave me a thrill.

Peeping from behind a cabinet was a putter! It was the type of club I would have liked to own. Nice and long in the shaft so that you needn't crouch too much at address, and slender enough to accentuate the weight in the head. Slowly back, against the ground, a smooth follow through.

"Your father tells me you play golf." My attention rushed back.

"Yes, sir," I said.

Mr. Hancock (that was his name) arose and I noticed that his left shoulder was higher than his right, tell-tale sign of the man who has putted for hours on end. He walked over to the corner, picked up the putter and handed it to me. Then he turned to his secretary The young lady knew exactly what to do. She went over to a cocktail cabinet, produced a tumbler, and laid it on the floor. Mr. Hancock took two golf balls from a drawer in his desk and rolled them towards my feet.

"Let's see what you're made of," he said.

The tumbler was eight feet away. The awkward length. Carefully I lined up, remembered the bits about not gripping too tightly, keeping close to the ground, going back and following through low and smooth.

My first putt slipped past. The second sweetly died in the glass.

That was the end of the interview.

"Good," said Mr. Hancock, "I'll write."

Instinctively I knew I'd made the grade. The secretary showed me out. A week later my father received a letter to say that a position was available.

At the end of the following term I left school, and became a member of the honorable company of week-end golfers.

I Play on the Office Team

IT'S NO USE pretending that I approved this interruption to my golf. Being away from the game for five days a week was rather like leaving home for the first time in my life.

In the early days, I took a rubber gripping device to work with me. This I squeezed with alternate hands while I was speaking on the telephone. One day, Mr. Hancock caught me at it. I'm not sure whether it was my hand exercising, or the fact that I was using the phone for the purely personal reason of fixing up a partner for the monthly medal. Whichever it was, I knew that the incident constituted the first positive step of my advancement in the brush-making firm. Fifteen years late, almost to the day, I was honored with a directorship and the more or less permanent captaincy of our Golf Section.

In the way it invariably does, time passed. I soon realized that the happy accident whereby Mr. Hancock's father and my grandfather chose the same school for their sons had made possible the one job in the world which need not jeopardize my golf.

Of those days, I can truthfully say that most rewards which I enjoyed were the direct outcome of honest sweat and toil, although not always my toil.

Nevertheless, I was usually involved and as an illustration I toss in the instance of our pneumatic interchangeable hairbrush.

From the day our firm launched this boon to barbers, the salesmen's order books were full. As a result of good business, we all got bonuses. Which meant I got my first matched-set of steel-shafted irons. Privately, I celebrate the great occasion every time my barber takes a fresh brush from the sterilizing cabinet. This first set of beautiful matched clubs was an important milestone in my life. Vividly I recall the circumstances.

On the Thursday before Easter Mr. Hancock had given a day off to seven of us. A hog-bristle importer from London had challenged our boss to a golf match. The game had developed into a team affair.

Our side was made up of fellows from the Management Department and three representatives, one having been especially brought in from Wales. We were to play on our home terrain; 36 holes, foursomes.

I don't know why I was listed to play as partner to the Boss. Maybe it was to please my father, but more than likely Mr. Hancock had heard that I was playing just a little inside my handicap and he needed the strokes. Anyway, I was thrilled at the prospect, and noticed that one or two of the girls in the office were observing me for the first time.

Apart from representing my golf club in one match when I had been brought in as a fifth replacement for a regular who had to be scratched, this was the first time I had been invited to play for anything, or anyone, anywhere.

You will appreciate my feelings.

Our opponents were a couple of queer cusses: the hog-bristle importer and his chief accountant. The latter was an old man who sniffed up huge quantities of snuff in the clubhouse, where Mr. Hancock had laid on cups of coffee as an agreeable preliminary.

The match was well organized and not the least of my surprises was to find that our Skipper had arranged that each player on both sides was to have a caddie. Although rather unnecessary for a strapping youth like me (whose light bag contained only six clubs), nevertheless the convenience was pleasantly adult and greatly appreciated.

Sketching in the game very lightly, I would start by saying that the Boss told me to take the first drive. This was a mistake, for at that precise moment I wasn't fit. Our opponents, as visitors, had been given the honor; and for his side the aged accountant had performed reasonably well. He grunted satisfaction, handed his driver to the caddie and fumbled for his snuff box.

My boss said: "Use this"—and handed me a new ball. I must have been standing to leeward of the old accountant bloke, for just as I was peeling the paper from the new ball, I was assailed by a cloud of snuff. I sneezed violently, once, twice—then there was a pause so I teed up. During my preliminary wiggle it happened again. "Wait a bit," said the Boss kindly. The sneezing didn't recur, but how was I to know it wouldn't? Folks were staring. I felt a complete fool.

Not surprisingly, that first drive of mine was nonsense. The ball nipped smartly along through long grass to the right for about twenty yards, hit a small roller, bounced jubilantly in the air, then plumetted with a clean splash into a water can. It was the sort of thing a trick-shot golfer would do at the end of his program.

Scarlet faced, hating myself, I went to retrieve the ball. "Don't bother," shouted the Boss, "the caddie'll get it."

I returned to the tee. Ours was the first game, so all members of both teams were there. Quietly, but without sympathy, they watched the fun.

The Boss played a beauty. In panic I moved off with the others to where our ball lay, awaiting my next shot.

This was the game and countryside I knew and loved. You would never have believed my antics that morning. I tried everything. Shorter swing, longer swing, two-knuckle grip, three-kunckle grip, four-knuckles. And when I'd run out of knuckles I tried something else.

I was sorry for the Boss. He had played beautifully, yet we were five down when we went in for lunch. I would not have believed I could play so badly. After each shot I told the others just that. Then I mumbled some diagnosis of what was wrong with my stroke. Only once was there a reply. The Boss said: "Only coroners have post mortems." I knew by his tone that I had better shut up.

The truth of the matter is that when you make a bad shot no one gives a tinker's cuss. The folks you are playing with couldn't care less if it's because you've quit with your left, dropped your right shoulder, or swallowed your uvula. To keep on saying what you've done wrong, and that you would "never have believed you could play so badly," is a frightful bore. I think it was on this occasion that I learned the great truth.

After a dozen holes I said nothing, simply suffered inwardly. But suffer I did and when we went in for lunch it must have shown on my face.

Our production manager was a Scot named Meiklejohn. I think he'd once been a golfer. In the friendliest way he put his arm around my shoulder. "Ye've been doon the long black tunnel, laddie," he said. "Never mind. Forget yersel' and maybe this afternoon . . ."

"Down the long black tunnel" was rather good.

After lunch, the others had port. I had an extra cider which I didn't much want, but perhaps it helped. My game greatly improved, and I took care to stand on the safe side of "Snuffy." At the 35th I holed a thirty-foot putt to give us a 2 and 1 victory.

This long putt of mine: everything about it was splendid. The ball dropped, the Boss yelled "Hoorah!", our opponents murmured "Good putt!", the caddies grinned, and I walked slowly over to the hole and retrieved the ball without speaking a word. Carefully planned, brilliant execution, success—but not achieved without strain. That was the effect I was after. The idea is to look as if the shot has taken something out of you, although, of course, you knew you could do it in a crisis.

We played four balls down the last fairway. Completely slap-happy, I outdrove the others and chattered my way towards the clubhouse.

Within a few days my wage envelope contained the bonus. How could I even consider using the cash for anything but golf?

That evening I was in consultation with the Pro about a new set of matched irons. Dad said it seemed an extravagance, but the Pro agreed I was doing the right thing. Later, when I mentioned to Mr. Hancock that I had invested my bonus in a matched set of irons, he said: "That's good. I like to see my young men use common sense."

It's All in the Feel

I HAD BEEN OUT with the Pro for many lessons. Also, of course, I had read books and magazine articles. The mechanics of the game were as clear to me as the guts of a glass clock. But what was far more important, I was beginning to appreciate the importance of *feel*. Here was something subtle and tremendously appealing.

Feel can't be photographed, nor seen, nor even described. This is the mystery element that has shackled me to golf for life.

A crusty old fellow—who, I learned later, was asked to resign from his previous club because he couldn't resist interfering with folk at play by telling them what they were doing wrong—once collared me on the practice ground.

"Feel the swing in your fingers," he said. I didn't catch on at first. Later it began to sink in.

This old chap carried on an endless vendetta with all professionals, including ours. It made things awkward. By listening to his theories, no doubt I encouraged him and I shouldn't have done this. But the stuff was a drug.

This is what he'd dispense: "It all starts in a button on the point of your left shoulder. That's the center of the circle. Your left arm and club are the radius. Start from the ball, go back as far as you can in comfort, winding your body like a spring. Then come right through again, making the imaginary line traced by your clubhead pure and free from bumps. Swing it down. *Feel* governs the speed. In fact, if you will only let it take over, *feel* will make the arc and do the whole job for you."

I learned a lot from these discussions. But one thing I couldn't understand—although it becomes clearer now: *If these great students of golf are right in their findings, why are they not all champions?*

I knew this old man for nearly twenty years. Yet, during the time we were friends, never once did his handicap move from 14. He entered competitions until he was eighty, then took umbrage because he couldn't get partners. I can't recall him ever winning. Why, if he knew the great secret, didn't his game improve? Never mind. If you are thoroughly addicted you'll know the answer.

Like all high-spirited people, my elderly friend had a temper which only youthful members like myself could possibly accept. One morning we met in the town. For no good reason, he addressed me stormily. We were on opposite sides of the road. "Hello, young fellow," he shouted, "where do you think you're going?"

"To play a game of golf," I replied. This seemed the right answer.

The old chap stood, legs apart, arms akimbo. He threw back his head and yelled: "Play? Game? Misnomers! Misnomers! Play? You don't *play* at golf! Game? What do you mean Game? That's a laugh!"

71

A woman looked around to see what was wrong. My friend stamped away, growling something or other to those in the vicinity.

This elderly apostle went out for nine holes on his eighty-seventh birthday, came back to the clubhouse, ordered tea, and then died before it arrived.

From my early days I have never underestimated the importance of competitive play. True addicts always support monthly medals, President's Cups, and the like. They never give up hope. Offer odds against him winning and you will find the addict bobbing up with his coin. What matter that he hasn't won a thing for ten years—this may well be the day. He goes further. Thinking the matter over, he is convinced that this most certainly *is* the day.

On past form he hasn't a chance. But you show me the man who actually believes *that* at breakfast time on a Medal day, and I'll show you a skunk.

Apart from competitions like Mixed Foursomes, the only tournament of importance that I've ever won was spoiled for me by my friends. The cup of success was knocked from my lips by those who should have been kinder.

It was on one of those days when everything went right. We were a big field playing a bogey competition in thick fog on a seaside golf course. My play was superb. Credit where credit's due, the caddie helped. Visibility was about fifty yards. My man—who knew every inch of the terrain—simply pointed me in the right direction and handed me a club. I just let fly and we walked on, through the fog, to where my ball always correctly landed. As can happen on those halcyon days, putts fell beautifully from all angles. It was so easy.

I countersigned my score card at 3 up. When we handed it in, the checker nearly had a fit! Nothing approaching that had so far come to hand. My friend and I inspected the lovely solid silver George III candlesticks which the winner was to receive that night at a reception being given by the Mayor.

Never have I felt so good. It was all over, bar the shouting. Through the luncheon room window we could see the last players finishing out on the 18th. It became positively clear that this was my day.

There was a snag which sent a slight shiver down my spine. Not much, but an irregularity on my score card could be disputable . . . Disqualification? The horrible thought crossed my mind and the bottom fell out of my stomach. "Have a drink," said a friend. It was tasteless. Until the checker said: "With 3 up, you've won easily!"

Even then, the sweet nectar of victory was dashed from my lips. Because I was dependent on my friends for transport, I missed the reception and the awarding of the prizes. A stooge came forward and, on my behalf, took the silver candlesticks from the Mayor. On my mantelpiece the candlesticks stand for all to see, but my undelivered acceptance speech hangs over them like a ghost.

I Lose the Touch

EVEN IN MY soul searching moments of truth, usually after I've been down "the long black tunnel," I would never admit that my game has not improved. In many ways, it has. Sometimes strokes sneak their way into a round quite inexplicably!

As a youth, I cracked long ones, but sometimes they snaked off to the right. Or else I wrapped the club around my neck and hooked the ball 200 yards to the left. It was great fun, but it was neither artistic nor scientific. The trouble is one can only assess golf in retrospect.

I have written of the elderly addicts who left an impression on my youth. There were youngsters as well. Scraggy was the name of a twenty-five-year-old fellow with whom I often played. He could hit the ball a mile, and I can declare without hesitation that he was the main reason why I came perilously close to suicide.

I will never regret the ordeal through which I passed. It was the same spartan medicine Stalin took when he walked naked in the snow to cure himself of tuberculosis. The lesson I had to learn was: not to covet that which belongs to my neighbor. In this case, it was Scraggy's ability to crack a really long one off the tee.

It came about this wise. Together we went for a

seaside golfing vacation. It was a revelation. I am prepared to go on record as saying I have never seen a golf ball hit further than I did during that summer.

Scraggy was tall and gangling, with big knobby hands. Normally he hit the ball far; but on this holiday something or other was harnessing all the power in his muscular frame and simply pouring it into the ball. He was winding up until the clubhead nearly touched the ground behind. At the top of the full pivot, his body was so far round that his back faced the tee box. After impact his follow-through was through and through, until two complete circles had been traced by his clubhead every time he drove the ball.

Looking back in an analytical way on this disastrous jaunt, I believe that on his first drive Scraggy just said to himself: "I'm going to beat the daylights out of this one." We all say that sort of thing from time to time. Then, when the ball is either badly hooked or topped, we cut out the nonsense and exercise restraint.

With Scraggy, his mighty swipe came off. After three such snorters the timing had clicked into place, confidence abounded, and he didn't think of anything—except turning on the heat. The extraordinary thing was that these colossal shots were dead straight. It was an extraordinary exhibition of super-energy hitting by a double-jointed giant.

I wouldn't have been human had I not tried to keep up with him. You know what happened. I got progressively worse. After three days my drives were ridiculous. The swing had vanished and in its place there was merely a disjointed, contrived punch.

On the fourth day, as a desperate measure, I refused to play with Scraggy and fixed a game with an elderly colonel, handicap 20. He beat me 6 and 4. Excepting for a short hole where I took a six iron, he outdrove me every time. My usual movement with the driver had completely gone. What was left was unworthy of a place on any golf course.

For me, of course, the vacation was wrecked. I returned to our home Pro, gray and dejected. Here was a kindly man, my friend. I poured out a troubled heart; then we worked in the net like slaves. We tried everything. In the past, he had always been able to help when things were wrong. This time, the virus was entrenched. After four long sessions, my master's patience was exhausted.

"If you're not going to do as I say, how do you expect me to effect a cure?" he said petulantly. I was doing my best and I told him so, almost in tears.

He knew I spoke the truth. "Let's go and have a beer, Sir," he said.

Until the tankards were nearly empty neither of us spoke. Then this kindly man put a hand on my shoulder. "Why not give the game a rest for a bit?" he said.

Would you ask a musician to forfeit his eardrums? Or a sculptor to chop off his fingers? Only they would know my feelings when I heard the Pro's monstrous proposal. Dumbstruck, I gradually realized the tragedy that had befallen my golf.

The kindly Pro spoke softly: "Your swing's paralyzed," he said. "It's screwed up with inhibitions. At first, the mechanism went wrong because you wanted to hit. Then you tried to put it right by experimenting. If you saw yourself now, you'd faint."

There was nothing I could say. In my heart I knew he was right. We sucked in more ale, then came the *coup de grace*. "Strictly speaking," said the maestro, "your present golf action is inferior to that of a beginner."

After years of effort, study, practice . . . at something I wanted to excel at more than anything in the world, I was worse than when I started!

I went off alone to think. The suggestion to give the game a rest was more than I could take. No, I must either persevere, until the malady burned its way out of my system—or to the devil with golf—I'd quit.

That night was crisis point.

Next day, I was in the hospital having my appendix removed.

Three weeks later, I was on the golf course, playing rather well.

The Elusive Mysteries of
Mac's Chipper

IN THOSE YOUTHFUL vigorous days I often noticed that, although anyone can have a bad spell of driving or putting, the man who plays chip shots really well seldom brings in a bad score card.

The pitch and run shots look so easy. So does putting for that matter. But tension and black magic can freeze the ball and prevent it from dropping into the hole. With the drive, things usually go wrong when we try too hard. The cunning short ones, when executed by a master, seems as safe and certain as Christmas.

From my observations, golfers who have the priceless gift of being able to play this match-winning shot are nearly always seniors. They have no length from the tee, but get good figures because they bundle three shots into two by producing gloriously accurate chips.

It's usually a shallow little arc, body perfectly still, nothing moving but the arms, and precious little give in the wrists. The exponent of the shot whom I remember best was one of the old school. He always played, winter and summer, in a gray alpaca jacket with the sleeves turned back at the wrists. He just went up to his ball, and if it was anything under thirty yards from the pin, you could count on a single putt.

For this match-winning shot, Mac used a club

which he called "m'chipper." The shaft was cut down hickory; the blade was angled like a No. 5 iron, but it was narrow and thin with sandpapering.

That club was a wonder! I played a few shots with it, and it always seemed to work. To start with, the feel was right. Somehow, you knew before the clubhead actually made contact that the weapon would be flush to the ball and go through smoothly. The more I thought about this wonder club, the more I became convinced that here was the answer, so far as I was concerned, to getting a low handicap.

One Sunday morning, in the locker room before the crowd arrived, I tackled Mac.

"I want a club like your chipper," I said.

Mac grinned. "So do a lot o' folk," he said.

"I wondered if I could get the Pro to make one like it. . . ."

"Couldn't," said Mac. "Impossible. But he can borrow it to try a copy."

The matter was arranged. Mac loaned me the club until the following Saturday, and I took it to the Pro.

A sad interview took place. "It's that head, Sir," said the Pro. "We'd never do it. . . . Your best chance is to find one like it in a junk shop."

Without success, I rummaged among old clubs in all manner of places.

The thing was becoming an obsession with me. The desire to possess a "Mac chipper" was no doubt accentuated by the difficulties in finding one.

One day, our Pro told me he could cope. He'd come across the head of an old jigger that might do the trick.

We borrowed Mac's club again to check up on weight and length of shaft, and in a day or two I took delivery.

Mac handled it first. I watched his face anxiously. He held the club aloft, then took one or two gentle swings at an imaginary ball on the floor. He handed the club to me. "I'll have my own," he said.

The Pro and I put the two clubs together. Apart from mine having the obvious look of a newly-fashioned job, they were identical. My heart was in my spiked shoes. I went out on the course and chipped for two hours. When I hit a good shot, it felt like an accident.

The failure stands in my locker. I have had neither the inclination nor the courage to give it public appearance.

Mac's passing was a sadness to us all. At the time, I most certainly wondered about the fate of his chipper. Maybe I'm callous. As a matter of fact, a day or two later, our Pro raised the matter.

How to set about getting it? As time passed, I knew my chances decreased. This was aggravating. More than ever I believed that the super chipped would make me invincible.

As it happened, the problem of how to get the club without being indelicate was solved. Mrs. Mac wrote to the club Secretary requesting that the contents of her late husband's locker be turned over to the Pro for sale or disposal as he considered appropriate. I happened to be present in the shop when the Secretary discussed the matter. The Pro glanced in my direction and winked. I heaved a sigh of thankful relief.

But for cruel fate, my golf worries and peptic ulcers

should have ended. Unfortunately, Mac's chipper was not in the locker, nor was it at his home. The club had mysteriously vanished, and we could find no feasible explanation.

The Pro was sympathetic. I daresay he had often suffered similar misfortunes; most golfers do. On my behalf, he made exhaustive inquiries, but he always drew a blank. Time passed and eventually the matter was forgotten. Mac's chipper, and the magic it contained, are gone forever.

The Mixed Foursome Tournament and How I Blew It

MEMORY PLAYS peculiar tricks. This is the only way I can explain why the chipper, so deadly from thirty yards, recalls my marriage.

When I was thirty, there were two girls in my life—Kate and Rosie. Kate was a pretty sound fourteen handicap with whom I played regularly in mixed affairs. I can't think how I met Rosie.

The most memorable game I had with Kate was when we reached the final of the Spring Mixed Foursome. What an occasion!

The female half of the opposition was a comely Irish gal who rivalled my Kate in all sorts of ways. They had played many ding-dong matches, their handicaps had lowered simultaneously. To describe this particular meeting as a needle-match would be an understatement. Kate had made it clear to me beforehand that only one result was possible.

The weather was sunny and warm—unlike the two lady players who were behaving as cozily as icicles. A fair crowd had turned out to watch the match; and I, for one, was not too blasé to appreciate the tense atmosphere.

As a matter of fact, it was my first final. . . . It was also my last. I mention this now, lest it appear that I am always engaged in these antics. I shall need excuses when you learn what happened!

The play, for a mixed foursomes final, was of reasonably high standard. Pointless to recount details, but we fought neck and neck, naturally becoming less talkative as the game proceeded. When they made good shots, the girls threw dagger-looks of congratulation at each other; the other guy and I (we'd been good friends for years) were dodging the sparks.

With only one hole to go, the match was even. To the death! The crowd, seemingly, had become partisan. They had formed into two distinct camps, and maybe this had an adverse effect on the two more sensitive male players.

I repeat: All square; one to go. Our honor; my drive. I hit it straight, but skied to the clouds. It was a fatal error. I shook my head with remorse. "Never mind, dear," Kate hissed.

The attractive side of the opposition looked happily pained. The male opponent took his stance, waggled normally—and sliced out of bounds!

I will dispense with the asides. These are the facts: the opposition played another ball—better this time, but that was three off the tee. Kate played ours—a peach, which finished thirty yards from the green. The opponents' approach finished a couple of yards nearer to the green than ours, but unless they performed a miracle by holing a twenty-five yard chip, *we had three for the match.* It was all over, but the shouting, and no doubt Kate could already see the trophy on her mother's sideboard.

Thirty smooth yards to go. My shot; anywhere on the green would do, but nicer to be near the hole. . . .

I took my wedge.

Go on, say it! That's right. I produced the father and mother of all foul-ups! The ball flew off crisply to the right, and finished well-plugged into the face of a bunker.

In a mood you can imagine, Kate waded into the sand and took a slash. The ball moved two inches— deeper!

My chance. The explosion was like an H-bomb, but when the cloud of sand had cleared the ball was still half buried.

Kate's turn again. Drawn and pale, she climbed the wall of sand, glowered at the ball for at least eight seconds—then with a hysterical little laugh, she stooped and picked it up.

I should never forgive myself for what I did to Kate that afternoon, but you can't go through life like that. All the same, the 18th has never seemed the same to me since that day.

The Case of that
Blankety-blank Bunker

ROSIE AND I were married the following April. We had
a lovely honeymoon in Devonshire near Westward Ho!,
a course I had not previously played. The flat, straight
fairways gave me an opportunity to persevere with my
long irons, keeping my head well behind the ball at impact and letting the right shoulder ride smoothly under
the chin.

Home again, and many matters awaiting attention.
The entry lists were up for two competitions. I had to
get down to a decision regarding additional weight in
my woods, and there was much talking to be done about
the bit of trouble caused by the Assistant Pro, who had
been seduced by one of the lady members.

The harmony of our club was seldom torn by serious discord. I was taking a keener interest in these
things now and was often part and parcel of all the
usual rumpi. Such things, I mean, as changes of steward-
ship, round robins, protests about the moss on the
greens, soap and paper shortage in the toilets, etc. As a
member of standing with a 14 handicap, I was in a position to make myself heard if the beer was flat, and what
I said about unraked bunkers is nobody's business.

It would be fair to say that our average of five
stewards a year merely reflects the normal turnover in

this category of club employee. The Secretary's letters of resignation were periodically read out by successive Captains at specially convened meetings, and the normal letters of nonacceptance were drafted—all mere trivia which seldom rippled the calm waters of the clubhouse bar.

Only once in those days do I recall a major crisis. This was the dastardly attempt to destroy our heritage, or as one member rather casually described the incident, "twaddle about filling up a hole."

Brief details herewith: When our course was originally laid out, hickory sticks were used to hit balls made of gutta-percha. A drive of 180 yards was pretty good. For that reason, the long cross-bunker on the 14th fairway, being about 250 yards from the tee, was a good trap for a poor second shot. Nowadays, however, when tigers whack the ball 250 yards, their straight drives are gobbled up in that bunker, and some long-handicap dubs are unduly grateful for this unfair advantage.

So our club formed itself into two camps: (1) Those who wanted the cross-bunker at the 14th filled in and remade further from the tee; and (2) those who did not wish to interfere with the original course architecture.

There was a wall immediately behind the 14th tee. But in any case putting the tee further back would not have solved the difficulty, for there was another storm involving the Women's Section. Their tee for this hole was well ahead, and long-driving tigresses could do themselves a bit of good by carrying the bunker. If it was moved forward, not only would the powerful ladies lose this advantage, but to make matters worse, they could also be trapped.

We therefore had the two camps: Tigers plus Lady dubs versus Tigresses plus Men dubs. The lineup was interesting.

To decide how best to deal with at least four petitions from members, an Extraordinary Committee Meeting was called. Committee members from both the Men's and the Ladies' Sections were convened.

A gathering of this description is a rarity in any golf club. Ladies are wanted only for odd jobs, like the decorations at Christmas, helping with table service on special days, or as ball-spotters for the Open Meeting. Other than on these occasions, the only times ladies are mentioned at the Men's Committee Meeting is when someone proposes that they should not be allowed on the course on Saturday mornings. This discussion is a hardy annual. Otherwise, they are neither consulted nor noticed.

The fact that they were in this up to their fair necks shows the magnitude of the affair. At first, the poor Secretary (who said he should not have this sort of worry at his time of life) had arranged for the Ladies' Captain and the Men's Captain to have an exploratory chat. Over a couple of martinis it was hoped the matter could be amicably settled.

Not on your life.

The Captains' informal talk took place in a corner of the lounge. I was sitting quite near, all ears. "Now perhaps you'll just listen to me . . ." said the Lady Captain, raising her voice. But her masculine counterpart didn't. He arose to his feet. "This haggling won't get us anywhere," he said.

They left the bar without finishing their drinks and we knew the battle was fully joined.

A day or two later the Extraordinary Joint Committee Meeting took place. As a result, almost immediately thereafter the Secretary instructed Old George, Head Greenkeeper, to fill in the cross-bunker on the 14th. No, it would not be replaced with another hazard, at any rate for the time being.

George toddled off with the three lads who made up the groundstaff.

By the weekend we were all surpised to see that the 14th had been turned into a flat and singularly uninteresting hole. An outcry of discontent spread like a forest fire. There was a general feeling of frustration, and maybe this was intensified by the fact that the Captain had chosen that particular weekend to be absent from the club with a slight indisposition.

On Monday morning, so we heard later, the Secretary put through a telephone call to the Captain's place of business.

"Thank God you're there, Sir!" said the Secretary, sounding like the brave commander of Tobruk when relief came. A crisis was shaking the very foundations of the club, he said. Members were in open revolt. Brigadier Loftus was playing merry hell and threatening resignation if some idiot didn't do something about the massacre of the 14th hole.

Probably it was mention of the fierce Brigadier (he played about four times a year and was always behind with his dues) that caused the Captain to phone the Club President.

Our President was seen at the club only when he took the Chair at the Annual General Meeting, or when his wife insisted he take the dog for a run. He was a kindly man who had been edged into the presidency because he looked the part, and because he commanded the respect that nearly always accompanies great wealth. He must have been surprised when the Captain asked him to take the reins and accept responsibility for what appeared to be the small matter of a bunker.

As it was, our President proved once again that a critical situation nearly always produces the right man. Our leader simplified the whole affair.

"Members don't want the bunker filled in? They prefer it as it was before?" asked the President, after the Captain had explained the complicated controversy.

"Well, yes, that's about it."

"Then there's no problem."

Given his strategic briefing, the Captain grasped the situation by the forelock, and issued crisp orders to the Secretary. Within hours, George and his horny-handed team were up-sodding, hole-making, and sand-spreading.

By the weekend, the old familiar hazard was back again, smiling broadly at whomsoever viewed it from the appropriate angle.

As could have been expected, an indignation meeting was called by the Lady Captain. She "deplored the unauthorized action regarding the bunker on the 14th fairway." In acid tones, she pointed out that a change had been approved in full Joint Committee. It was irregular (and rather discourteous) for the Captain of the Men's Section (without consultation with those who only wanted to be helpful) to have the bunker restored to what it was before the meeting had arranged for it to be filled in, pending a further decision regarding a new bunker to be sited in a position to be determined later blah blah blah. . . .

The meeting agreed that the whole thing was scandalous. The Secretary was asked to instruct the groundstaff accordingly.

The bunker was filled in, and although the turfing had a quick-change-do-it-yourself appearance, the Lady Captain was satisfied.

At this point, once again, the President came into the picture. He scribbled a note to the Secretary announcing that he had lost his wedge, a venerable club to which he was greatly attached. Could a search be made, please.

The Secretary, assuming a not unfamiliar expression, explored locker rooms and elsewhere. He was about to telephone to the President, expressing regret, when Truth suddenly dawned! In a wave of cold panic he realized where the President had left his damned wedge.

Following the Captain's request for Presidential help over the troublesome bunker decision, and after orders had been given to open up the hole again, the President had become interested. He had personally supervised the excavation! To show Old George that he knew what was wanted, and by way of demonstrating, he played a few shots from the new/old bunker. The Secretary was there at the time and mildly applauded when the old man hacked one out. He remembered perfectly, also, that when one of the President's practice balls refused to leave the sand after four mighty blows, the old boy had tossed aside his wedge and stamped out of the bunker in disgust. There was the answer to the missing club! The Lady Captain, restoring the status quo, had somehow or other buried the President's wedge!

The tragedy was explained to the Head Green-keeper, who shouted to his team. "Open her up again," he said, and the bulldozer scooped and scraped.

The wedge wasn't in the sandy grave. Weeks later, it was found in the President's greenhouse.

The bunker was never tampered with again. So far as I know, it's still there.

I Toy with the Idea of Giving Up the Game

CHARACTERISTICS AND landmarks on one's home course become hallowed in time. We are all sticklers for convention and hate to see changes. Age is "a durned nuisance," as Will Rogers used to say, but in golf, nice things sometimes come late.

Years slip by and we may find ourselves in the Senior Golfer's Division. This pleasant state of affairs offers comfort to those who are eligible.

For your own advancement in the Senior Division, there is little you can do. A low handicap may be out of reach. Yet, by a certain kind of service to others, you can greatly increase their golfing stature. This device is reciprocal. If you are an accepted Senior, others will do the right thing by you.

Here's what I mean: Start of a game; you are on the tee. A member of your foursome has just driven badly. Those on the tee who will follow your foursome are youngsters, sturdy chaps who can all hit the ball a mile. They will not comment on your or your friend's puny drive, but they may sneer, inwardly. As a Senior, you must say to the tiger standing nearest: "He'll still get his bogey!" You speak *sotto voce,* in confidence, giving the impression that your friend is so deadly with approaches and putts that it doesn't matter whether his

drive is good or bad. Put it over properly and the youngster will surely be impressed.

You will have given your fellow Senior a desirable
buildup. The youngster will tell his pals, and after-
wards in the bar, you will know by their respectful attitude that a reputation has been created. Your friend
may even be pointed out—"There's one of the finest
short-game players in the club. A hard man to beat. . . ."
These things get around.

The Senior Golfers' Division is a brotherhood for
mutual uplift. A kind of prestige restorer. But, of course,
you are entirely dependent on others. Say about them
what you would wish them to say about you. Just that.

The only qualifications you require are a slight
stoop, grey hair at the temples, and at least one old club.
The latter you always carry, bringing it out for match-
winning shots on rare and appropriate occasions. Its
use is always accompanied by the casual comment that
your grandfather (using the same club) was deadly.
Employ the patter skillfully, and those with whom you
play will only remember the good shots. That is another
of golf's delightful compensations.

As stated, age is not the most important factor in
Senior golf. I joined the brotherhood when I was about
forty-five. In golf, you establish your category by the
company you keep. My regulars were mostly elderly,
serious chaps, who suffered just as many sleepless nights
and who fretted as much as I did because of golf addiction.

There was the Doc, with a slice that had been established for at least a quarter of a century. He never

had Surgery on Thursday afternoons, but his diagnosis problems on the golf practice ground were as difficult as anything he attempted with thermometer and stethoscope. "The new antibiotics won't cure this," he said gloomily, as his drives crescented off to the right.

Doc's regular partner was a prickly little man whom we called the Colonel because he looked like a caricature of one. Excepting on the greens and on the tees, Doc and the Colonel never met on the course. The Colonel's tight little hook was just as stubborn as Doc's slice. Apart from normal habit and politeness, there was no reason why one need wait on the tee while the other drove off. Either could follow his ball without getting in the way of the other's drive.

My usual partner was an addict who affected a dour phlegmatic role, pretending he could either take golf, or leave it alone. After our game when we discussed the next meeting, my man would say: "I shan't come if it's raining. The game's not worth getting wet for." He couldn't care less about golf; at least, that was the impression he liked to give.

Once, when the rain didn't stop for a week, and three of the greens were lakes, ours, was the only foursome on the course. We wore every shred of waterproofing that was available. Then prior to risking it, we paused in the doorway of the locker room. A stream swirled at our feet, and the rain fell straight down in long silver pencils. "What are we waiting for?" said my partner, and pushed us out into the storm.

Like my friends, I gradually became an accepted Senior, and I must say it's made a difference. We notice it with the Steward, more than with the Pro or ground staff.

Herbert, who dispenses the club drinks and will chat the most utter nonsense with anyone so inclined, has never struck a golf ball in his life. I would go further. I doubt whether he has ever watched a shot being played. Possibly he knows the general idea is to hit a small white ball into holes, but I'm sure that is as far as it goes. And Herbert couldn't care less. You can tell him anything. Also, you can count on it being repeated.

"I understand the Colonel had a fine round this morning," says Herbert, and we suspect that our friend has dropped the right kind of hint. Having played with the Colonel we know how he performed, but we sagely nod our heads and murmur "Incredible!" That's enough for Herbert. He passes on a long graphic description, and the Colonel's stock rises to the sky.

That sort of thing can happen to anyone in the Senior Division. We've perfected our technique and the Steward, for one, has no way of knowing that we are not all champions.

Like other things in life, being a Senior is all right when folk are there to cheer, but sometimes in the long, gray hours before dawn, when you are alone with your thoughts, there's a shiver. Mostly it comes after the age of fifty, when you first begin to doubt whether you will ever get your handicap down to scratch from, say, 12. You ask yourself—What's it all about anyway?

The icy finger poked into my vitals on my fifty-fifth birthday. It was a ghastly experience, as if my veins had suddenly been drained of blood and filled with cold tea.

My attitude towards golf had changed.

"It's only a game," I actually said. "Why not treat the game as relaxation? Aren't there other things in life?" Of course!

I'd been a fanatical fool. In the future, I would balance things out in reasonable proportions. Look around for something solid.

To celebrate my fifty-fifth milestone, my wife and I had dined out. In three days, we were due to leave on our summer vacation. I had arranged a two-weeks tour of the Scottish courses. My wife doesn't play golf. I'd explained how she'd love the scenery. As we returned from our birthday dinner, I said: "What about scratching Scotland, and doing Juan-les-Pins?"

"There's no golf there," said my missus.

"We can bathe," I said. "Nice excursions. . . ."

My wife made no comment, but she shot a quick glance in my direction. Our tour of the Scottish courses had been planned for weeks. Mountains, lochs, and so on—all came into it.

We walked along for a while, then my wife spoke. "Anything wrong at the office?" Her tone was low and serious. I had the impression that she thought I was depressed.

I laughed and explained how I had suddenly seen the light and changed my whole attitude towards golf. "Saturday afternoons, sometimes maybe, for exercise."

"No Sunday foursome?"

"Once in a while, perhaps. . . . "

We reached home and my wife said: "I'm putting a couple of aspirins in your coffee."

That night, I slept like a dead man until the alarm went off at six-thirty. Then I made my own breakfast, and hurried off to the club. It was Captain's Day. I had an early start, but first I wanted an hour on the practice ground with a new driver.

That year the competition for the Captain's Prize was eighteen holes, match play. I returned a net 70—which included a 7 on the lethal last hole. I could describe every shot of that round, although it happened years ago. A pleasant memory!

One of our strong young men did a 68, so I didn't get the prize, but in my mind there was no doubt who was the winner.

My golf that day was impeccable. The new driver worked beautifully, and possibly for the first time, I found the sweet spot on my old putter.

The Americans always say the quality of the last shot is the payoff. They're right, of course. During this outstanding round my putter worked as never before. Nothing dramatic or lucky, but at least six putts between five and twelve feet which poured smoothly up to the hole and died. So useful.

The Captain's prize, a set of good china, would have been taken home to my wife, but for the tragedy on the 18th.

My nerve didn't snap, and this is important. On that day Gene Sarazen, one of the greatest bunker players of all time, could have taken a 7. A nameless oaf had left a deep gash in the sandy wall of the bunker by the green and there my ball chose to nestle. As on a previous occasion, for me it was Waterloo.

97

Naturally, I started home crestfallen. The Pro came to the door of his shop as I passed. "Bad luck," he said. "I knew you had it in you."

I went home glowing. The Pro *knows* I have it in me! Isn't that a wonderful thing to remember!

Next day we began our glorious tour of the Scottish courses.

The Ineffable Mystery of Putting

I MENTIONED THE sweet spot on my old putter. Those of you who know the feeling will appreciate my efforts to enjoy the sensation more often. I wanted to insure a mechanical action which would bring the sweet spot flush to the ball every time. Slow, short back, against the ground, and through on the same straight line. That's the way it's done.

For a month I putted really well, and it became palpably clear that if a chap can sink everything under ten feet it shouldn't be difficult to break 80 on any golf course. I mean, for a normal citizen of 12 handicap.

Master the putt and the other shots become easy, because you don't press—knowing that you may easily gain a stroke against a chap who can't putt. For about a year, that was the theoretical background of my competitive golf.

To reach the stage of perfection required with my putter, I worked hard in the evenings, until my wife pointed out a kind of long straight milky way that was beginning to show on the dining room carpet.

I wish I could honestly report that this intensive study did the trick. Actually, I deteriorated.

Putting is as fugitive as a back itch. It is a fantastic truth that, no matter how much you labor, your skill may actually diminish. Sometimes a change will put it right. For two or three outings my new stick served me fairly well, but I always carried the old putter along, too —like the lady who had two watches, one without hands which she carried for the tick.

The routine was aggravating. For a while, a new putter would work. Then it went off. Then on again. . . . I positively knew that if I left one of my putters in the locker that would be the day it was blessed with magic. Each of these clubs was as temperamental as an overbred race horse. They had to be treated like children, and there is no doubt that any mothering instincts I possess were fostered and stimulated by the extraordinary relationship that existed between me and my putters.

Some putters we love as cherished dear ones. Others are hated with a ferocious venom that seldom abates, even after the putter in question has made amends by holing out some long ones.

I once saw a man toss a putter away, saying: "There isn't another decent putt left in it."

By far the best true story I've heard was told by Ted Ray.

In 1903, they played the Open Championship at at St. Andrews. That was the year James Braid pulled it off, despite close pursuit by J. H. Taylor, who was defeated by one shot. When J. H. missed a short putt on the 18th, which meant the championship, he was so angry that he flung his putter over the heads of the crowd and strode away in disgust. A little boy retrieved the evil implement and promptly sold it.

Fifty-five years later, the man who had given the little boy a sixpence for Taylor's putter, was visiting Westward Ho! Sitting outside the clubhouse was the great J. H. Taylor himself. The man went over and introduced himself.

"You won't remember me, Mr. Taylor," he said, "but more than half-a-century ago I was lucky enough to see you play in the Open Championship in St. Andrews."

Taylor said something appropriate and the man continued: "I think you will recall missing a short putt that lost you the championship, Sir?" Taylor nodded grimly. " . . . and do you remember being so angry that you threw your putter away?" Taylor nodded again.

"Well, Sir," said the man, "a little boy retrieved your club and I bought it for sixpence. I've used the putter ever since, and my friends say it has served me well. Now, Sir, I've come to Westward Ho! and I'd like to return your property."

With this pretty speech the man produced the club and graciously offered it to the original owner.

J. H. arose to his feet, grabbed the putter and flung it away. "You can keep the damn thing!" he said.

The Story of Ben's Quaich

I ALWAYS HAD a lot of time for the eccentrics. Completely dedicated, it was natural for them to get pleasure by spreading the gospel according to St. Andrews.

There was one chap whom I never met. He was a legend. I suppose the story has improved with retelling but roughly the facts are as follows: Ben loved in a village about eight miles from the golf club and to get there he used his bike. He was popular enough in a quiet way, and a keen golfer.

No one knew much about Ben's business, nor his home life. It had been said that Mrs. Ben was a battle-axe who cared nothing for golf. She had never been seen at the club.

One day, it is recouted, Ben and his spouse had words, although how anyone could know what transpired in these private circumstances is a mystery. The row was about Ben going off to golf.

"Wasting your time when you ought to be weeding the garden," was what Mrs. Ben was said to have said about Ben's life work. She flayed him mercilessly. "I don't know what you do there," she said, adding: "You never win anything!"

Cycling back from the club that evening Ben saw a nice piece of old silver in a junk shop window. We have all heard of anglers who make purchases at the fish store so that they don't return emptyhanded, but I had never been told of a golfer who "won" a trophy by buying it from a shop.

The piece of silver was yellow and elderly. A card said THIS QUAICH TWO POUNDS, but what really took Ben's eye, and probably put the naughty idea into his head, was the sight of three letters engraved appropriately on a smooth panel. They were "N.G.C."

A *quaich* is a Scottish porridge bowl and it is unlikely that they are often wrought in silver for use at table. These special ones usually register golfing conquest. They are sprinkled all over the country in trophy cabinets.

"N.G.C.?" Ben wondered what the letters stood for. He knew all the golf clubs for miles around. Nothing fitted.

Obeying an impulse, Ben bought the quaich, had it polished in the shop and, with a neat parcel, returned to his wife.

Vanity? Maybe, but I prefer to think otherwise. Ben, so they say, was a kindly man. I like to think that he took the quaich to his wife because he felt that perhaps it would sweeten his home life a little if his lady realized that golf wasn't simply a waste of time. Also, no doubt, he wanted her to be proud of him. After all, that is human.

Ben's quaich idea worked beyond his wildest hopes. The trophy was examined and admired by one for whom golf had suddenly become worthwhile. In fact Ben wasn't quite prepared for the questions. How did he win it? What sort of a competition? What did N.G.C. stand for? Shouldn't his name be engraved somewhere? Ben's wife was pleasingly excited.

No doubt Ben warmed to his subject—the patter would be easy—and when his wife actually kissed him, saying: "You *are* a real golfer," the hero turned away with a modest: "Oh, it was nothing."

Ben answered all the questions adequately. He had won a simple stroke competition. "N.G.C." stood for Northern Golf Club. This didn't need elaborating. His wife was satisfied and proud.

Next day was Sunday. I am quite sure that Ben had enjoyed his usual four-ball, but on his return the trouble started. A strange young man was in the house. "This is Mr. Biggin, from the *Clarion*," said Mrs. Ben. "Mrs. Rosewood, next door, told him about you winning the golf quaich."

"Congratulations, Sir," said the young man, shaking Ben's hand. "I'd like a few facts. It isn't every day that we have a golf champion in the village."

Imagine Ben's feelings. He had never expected his wife to chatter to the neighbors! In the village there lived another member of the golf club. Supposing he should hear the story! It had to be squashed.

"I prefer no publicity. It was a very small competition," said Ben.

"Oh, come, Sir. Nothing vulgar. Just a few lines. I've got a nice photo of the trophy, but I'd like one of you standing by it, with Madam, perhaps. . . ."

As quickly as possible Ben got rid of the fellow. But he was a zealous young man and when the local news sheet was delivered a day or two later, things couldn't be worse. There was an illustration of the quaich, plus an account of Ben's golfing success—as told by his wife! Ben's modesty was stressed, which somehow made the whole thing seem more frightful.

The *Clarion* was a small country newspaper with a circulation mainly in the villages to the west of Ben's home. The golf club was to the east. Ben hoped fervently that the paper would never be seen by his golfing friends. He even went around the countryside on his bike buying up every copy he could find. This may not have been a good idea either, for when he bought the four copies in the rack at the village Post Office the girl immediately suspected vanity and naturally did her bit of gossiping.

For two weeks Ben made the supreme sacrifice. He stayed away from the club. This perplexed his wife. "Won't they think it funny," she said, "now that you have won the quaich . . .?" She probably likened it to getting up from a poker table, cash in hand when you're way ahead.

Within a month the inevitable happened. There was a telephone call from the other club member who lived in the village. Ben knew the game was up. "About that quaich . . ." said Ben. He had made his decision.

Fortified by strong drink, Ben laid bare his heart. The club member listened patiently.

To Ben's relief, the man seemed to understand. He promised not to mentioned it to any living soul.

There, so far as the golf club was concerned, the matter rested. At least, for about three weeks, which is the usual time for a story like this to get circulated.

At no time was Ben actually confronted with the deception by any member. Possibly his popularity increased, or would have but for a certain development which ultimately led to Ben's departure from the neighborhood.

One day, a man came to Ben's house. Fortunately, Mrs. Ben was out shopping. The visitor was an official of that popular ancient institution known as the Nottingham Goose Fair. "About that quaich . . ." he started.

Reviewed in retrospect, I don't suppose Ben's deception permanently improved his home life. Nor would one imagine that his wife looked more tolerantly on golf addiction. Nevertheless, Ben can rightly claim to have been instrumental in finding the missing trophy of the Nottingham Goose Club.

The Addiction is Beyond Cure

TO THE HOARY old golfers of the Senior Division, club handicaps seldom bear any relation to the standard of play. They mean little. Yet, in a way, the quality tag is important.

According to the records, Old Fred, who plays in our Thursday afternoon foursome, is 14. Over the years, we have played hundreds of rounds together, and I would doubt if he has ever broken a hundred. But watch out for a crisp retort if anyone suggests that his handicap should be revised. No one would dream of mentioning the subject. Certain things just aren't done.

Like the rest of us, Fred no doubt sweated the strokes off, one at a time, from 24 to 14, in the far distant past. Coming down may have taken years. Perhaps there was a fluky medal round or two. I don't know. But the reduction took place long ago, in an aura of great anxiety and possibly happiness. Tampering with Fred's handicap would be like jazzing up an ancient Gothic window.

Fred never enters tournaments. He hasn't taken a card out for years, nor is he likely to ever do so. The respectable figure on the handicap board, where everyone can see it, is all he has left.

At seventy-nine years of age, my friend never plays

with strangers. Strokes aren't discussed in our foursome. We know that Fred gets one at the long 6th, one at the 11th, one at the 13th, and one at the 17th, if we don't walk in earlier.

And yet, in direct contrast to Fred's noble attitude, we know one or two Seniors who have actually asked for handicap revisions, claiming that with the passing of years they can no longer play to 12 or 14, or whatever it is.

They usually get what's coming to them!

A disagreeable retired lawyer, who shall be nameless, filled a gap in our four the other day. He seemed to like our company, and was pleased to be considered first reserve to take the place of a possible absentee.

When we reached the 11th, he said: "I don't give strokes here now." We looked at him in amazement. The 11th is the hardest hole on the course. We always get strokes at the 11th.

"I've had my handicap changed." He spoke with smug satisfaction, instead of horror at going down the slippery slope. The retired lawyer will never play with us again.

How different from Fred! Ask for a handicap revision? Why, he'd sooner lose his left arm.

I once heard the Secretary politely ask him how he was playing. Maybe it was a loaded question to give Fred a chance to suggest a handicap increase. At any rate, I think Fred suspected that. Did he jump at the opportunity? Not on your life.

"Never played better," said Fred. "Recently, I've knocked off about eight strokes a round." He didn't mention that for the past six months our foursome has cut out the last two holes.

For years I have considered Sunday morning the highlight of golf. Now, I am not so sure. We tough old Seniors who play slightly abridged rounds each Thursday afternoon view the occasion as seriously as it deserves. For instance, last Summer we sent a round robin to the Committee on the subject of cutting the greens.

Throughout the sunny months the greens on our course receive attention twice a week—on Fridays, so that they are in good condition for weekend play, and on Mondays. By the time it gets to Thursday, the greens are as whiskery as an old sailor.

We signed a document pointing out that Friday and Monday cutting was bad, because this divided the week unevenly. Unmolested, the grass grew all day Tuesday, Wednesday and Thursday. Surely this was incorrect, since the other noncutting days were only Saturday and Sunday. Would not Tuesday be a better cutting day than Monday?

The reply came pronto. No, the groundsmen could not cut greens on Tuesdays. That was the ladies' match day. In a pleasant note we thanked the Committee, emphasizing our unwillingness to interfere with the ladies, but couldn't their match day be changed to Wednesday? No, it couldn't, came the response. On Wednesdays, the stores closed early. Therefore it was out as a match day.

Then came the sting which ceased all further correspondence. In his last salvo, the Secretary explained that cutting the greens on Tuesdays had been considered, with a change of ladies' match day to Thursdays, but a *certain men's Thursday foursome was so deeply rooted that the change was undesirable!*

This will give you an idea of the attitude towards our foursome. We have tremendous stature.

Approaching the sear and yellow, I find myself clinging more to the gentle compensations of the game. Admittedly, we lose yardage from the tee, but with retirement one gets down to devising a sound short game. Master this aspect and you can be a centenarian trophy collector.

A good thing about the passing years is the fact that as each twelve-month period slips away, it becomes a stroke easier to play eighteen holes to your age. Like every other addict, I have that secret ambition.

On his seventy-fifth birthday, it is alleged that James Braid went round at Walton Heath in seventy-five strokes. James Sherlock is reputed to have done an 80 at Hunstanton during his eighty-first year. This high pinnacle of golf is something denied the young tigers.

At Pine Valley, one of the most difficult golf courses in the world, a man named Platt started his round 3, 3, 1, 3. Then he stumbled into the clubhouse. Six strokes inside par! He couldn't continue because the strain was too great. Platt lived on for many golfing years, no doubt wondering whether that was the day he would have broken 50! The law of averages and precedence were heavily loaded against that happening, but the color red once came up twenty-one times consecutively on a Monte Carlo roulette wheel!

WE'RE JUST
MIXED-UP
KIDS UNTIL
THE
END

A SHEAF OF CARTOONS

"NOW, THIS IS THE POSITION I WANT YOU
TO GET — BUT YOU MUST BE COMPLETELY
RELAXED..."

"KEEP YOUR HEAD DOWN!"

"GLADYS, CAN YOU HEAR ME? I'VE
QUALIFIED!"

"I SAID **BRASSIE!**

"IT HAPPENS THAT I *DO* MIND IF YOU JUST STAND THERE AND TRY TO PICK SOMETHING UP"

"AWKWARD, OLD CHAP, BUT I SUPPOSE IT'S
THE SORT OF THING WE MUST EXPECT IN
THE AUTUMN..."

"OH, LOOK! IT'S GONE INTO **MY** BUNKER!"

"SO THIS IS WHAT GOES ON! — WHILE I'M AWAY WORKING LIKE A SLAVE TO GET MY HANDICAP DOWN..."

"PORT OR BRANDY, SIR?"

"BUT COLONEL, SHOULDN'T WE FIND MY BALL FIRST, *THEN* GET TO KNOW EACH OTHER BETTER?"

"I STILL THINK BABY WOULD BE HAPPIER IN HIS PRAM..."

"WHAT DO **YOU** KNOW ABOUT FIGHTING ADVERSITY?"

"I SOMETIMES WONDER IF WE'VE GOT THE
RIGHT MAN AT THE HELM..."

"BUT SURELY THERE MUST BE DOZENS OF GOLFERS WHO CAN'T REMEMBER HOW MANY THEY TOOK AT THE 7th..."

"YOU CAN GO NOW — THERE'S NO ONE IN THE BUNKER"

"I'VE LOST MY PIVOT!"

"I DOUBT IF WE'LL GET ANOTHER HOLE FROM THIS BATTERY, SIR."

"SOMETIMES, I THINK YOU TRY **TOO** HARD — WE MUST CONCENTRATE ON NOT CONCENTRATING..."

"THERE'S NO NEED TO EXAGGERATE!"

"THERE IT GOES AGAIN, WILLY BOY—YOUR STRAIGHT ONE!"

"THE WEAKNESS IN YOUR PUTTING IS
FUNDAMENTAL—YOU CAN'T AIM!"

"ANY OTHER MAN CAN ENJOY A NICE QUIET GAME OF GOLF — **YOU** HAVE TO HAVE A SWING THEORY!"

"— AND WE DIDN'T COME TO PARIS TO WONDER WHETHER YOU COULD CLEAR THE ARC DE TRIOMPHE WITH AN EIGHT IRON SHOT!"

137

"LET'S FACE IT, OLD CHAP, GOLF JUST ISN'T **YOU**".

"I WOULD SAY A SIX IRON SHOT..."

"WE'RE NOT DOING BADLY — THERE'S THE CLUBHOUSE!"

"FORE!"

"DON'T FORGET TO TELL ME WHEN TO KEEP MY DARNED MOUTH SHUT..."

"HE SAID I COULDN'T REACH THIS GREEN WITH MY DRIVE!"

"WEDGE"

"— BUT YOU JUST TRY AND GET HIM TO PADDLE WITH THE CHILDREN...!"

"IT'LL TAKE HIS MIND OFF THE STRAIGHT
LEFT ARM THEORY."

"THIS SHOULD BE GOOD FOR A LAUGH!"

"JUST HOW I LIKE IT — NO CROWDS ON THE FIRST TEE..."

"IF YOU DON'T WANT TO PLAY ME WHY
NOT SAY SO?"

"FOUR ROUNDS OF GOLF AT THE WEEKEND, CARPET PUTTING AT NIGHT... AND ALL YOU CAN SAY IS THAT I DON'T UNDERSTAND!"

"FOUR ROUNDS OF GOLF AT THE WEEKEND, CARPET PUTTING AT NIGHT... AND ALL YOU CAN SAY IS THAT I DON'T UNDERSTAND!"

ALPHABETICAL INDEX
OF ILLUSTRATIONS

Alphabetical Index of Illustrations